T0042327

The Corn
That Kay Grew

Susan Long
Illustrated by Jacqui Grantford

This is the corn
that Kay grew.

Farm Fresh Corn

This is the truck
that carries the corn
that Kay grew.

This is the store
that sells the corn
that Kay grew.

This is the worker
who stacks the corn
that Kay grew.

Carrots

Corn

h Corn

Spinach

This is the shopper
who buys the corn
that Kay grew.

This is the father
who cooks the corn
that Kay grew.

This is the family
that eats the corn
that Kay grew.

This is the corn
that Kay grew!

16